Making Music to the Lord

BRINGING RENEWED WORSHIP TO YOUR LOCAL CHURCH

Anne Coles

With contributions from
Neil Bennetts, Ed Pask, David Pytches, Matt Redman

new wine international publishing

Text copyright ©2001 Anne Coles. Neil Bennetts. Ed Pask. David Pytches. Matt Redman. Andy Rushton.
The authors assert the moral right to be identified as the authors of this work.

First Published in Great Britain in 2001 by
new wine international publishing
PO Box 176, Berkhamsted, Herts , HP4 3FH, England.
ISBN 1-902977-10-6

First Edition 2001
10 9 8 7 6 5 4 3 2 1 0

Acknowledgements
All scripture quotations are taken from the Holy Bible New International Version, copyright
© 1973,1978,1984 by International Bible Society. Used with permission of Hodder and Stoughton a member of the Hodder Headline Group. All rights reserved. 'NIV' is a registered trade mark of International Bible Society.
UK trade mark number 1448790

Appendix copyright St Barnabas Church North Finchley & Andy Rushton and used with permission.

A catalogue record for this book is available from the British Library

Type set & cover design, Mike Thorpe, Design Chapel
Printed in Great Britain by Gemini Print Services

CONTENTS

Introduction

1.   Characteristics of Biblical Worship   6

2.   Values in Worship   10

3.   Introducing Renewed Worship in a Traditional Setting   12

4.   The Worship Leader   16

5.   The Band   19

6.   Church Leadership and the Musical Director **David Pytches** 21

7.   Leading Worship **Neil Bennetts**   26

8.   Choosing The Right Songs   32

9.   Using the Band to Best Effect **Ed Pask**   36

10. Sound Reinforcement (P.A.)   43

11. Criticism and how to deal with it   46

12. Singing in tongues   48

13. Songwriting **Matt Redman**   51

     Conclusion   55

     Appendix - Operating a sound system   57

INTRODUCTION

Worship is the heart and core of the life of the Christian believer and therefore of the body of believers - the church. Worshipping the Almighty God is what we are made for and our life and work only makes sense in the context of that worship. AW Tozer said: I am of the opinion that we should not be concerned about working for God until we have learned the meaning and delight of worshipping him. A worshipper can work with eternal quality in his work.

Our sung worship is one of the outward expressions of that life of worship. Many of us have been transformed as we have responded to God together in singing; we have experienced His holy presence again and our lives have been renewed and restored. This is why so many people who come to New Wine conferences say that the worship times have been the highlight for them. We believe that this should also be the regular experience of the local church.

Spiritual revivals have always been characterised by a renewed outpouring of songs of worship and the church today has been blessed with a renewal in its worship. God's truth is unchanging but as the Spirit of God moves in each successive generation, Christians will find their own ways of expressing that truth. 'The truth stands in the Bible but the tunes change with the times!'

Many churchgoers ask why we are not singing the old traditional hymns with the organ and choir anymore. For many that have been brought up in the church, this is what is familiar and it has been a blessing to them. We should not deny them a service where they can worship in a way that brings them into the presence of God. Of course there are still many churches where this is the only style of worship.

However, we live in a fast-changing culture and that change has also affected music. In the two hundred years up to the middle of the last century, the development of music in popular culture had been slow and this was reflected in church music as well.

In the 1950s a new type of music burst on the scene - rock and roll, with guitars (even the boy next door could buy, learn and play one!) and drums (the beat was new, signalling the rise of a new generation).

This new music found a resonance around the world. With the development of the modern communication network, 'rock' music has fast become the musical language of a New World generation. As in Jesus' day the Roman Empire, with its common language, enabled the rapid spread of the gospel, so the global appeal of today's popular music has become the means of the creation of worshipping communities around the world. Across cultures from East to West and North to South the same worship songs are sung. Instruments indigenous to one culture are used by the local church at worship - and then picked up by another culture! This is particularly the case for percussive and rhythmic instruments.

As someone has once said, the church is the one organisation that exists for the benefit of its non-members. The world needs to recognise and appreciate the musical 'language' of our worship in order to be drawn into the church and not feel alienated. In rock music, in all its many forms, we have an international music language. Let's encourage each other to make the appeal of Jesus Christ to this generation in a language that it can understand and use!

Equally, the world is longing to be inspired by the worship of the church. Throughout the centuries it has often been Christian worship music that has both uplifted the spirit and set the standard for the world. We need to give God the very best we can, and aim for the highest standards in our worship. We try to give some practical help here in order to achieve this.

Each generation and culture will find new expressions of worship. Experience shows however that making changes in the worship style of any given church can be something akin to navigating an obstacle course! In this booklet we hope that you will find some helpful guidelines and advice for bringing this renewed worship to your local church.

1 Characteristics of Biblical Worship

A heart activity

Although worship is an outward, visible and audible activity, the Bible makes it clear that God is looking for worship from the heart.

> *I Sam 16:7 But the LORD said to Samuel, "Do not consider his (Saul's) appearance or his height, for I have rejected him. The LORD does not look at the things man looks at. Man looks at the outward appearance, but the LORD looks at the heart."*

> *Isaiah 29:13 The Lord says: "These people come near to me with their mouth and honour me with their lips, but their hearts are far from me. Their worship of me is made up only of rules taught by men."*

It's obviously not good enough just to sing the words, know the tunes or put on a 'holy' expression. The words of our lips have to be backed up by the actions of our lives. This involves both repentance and purity.

This means that the church needs to be taught the 'whole counsel of God' - the story of salvation and how it affects the believer's life. It is no good just singing the songs of renewal if the church is not being taught how to be renewed. Further than that, we need to be encouraging each other to put into practice what we learn

> *Phil 4:9 Whatever you have learned or received or heard from me, or seen in me - put it into practice. And the God of peace will be with you.*

Developing open, caring and accountable relationships in small group settings will help here.

Praise and thanksgiving

Praising God for who He is and thanking Him for what He has done have always been an integral part of Biblical worship. Moses and Miriam led the people of Israel in jubilant songs of praise and thanks after God had rescued them from the Egyptians by bringing them through the Red Sea on dry land.

Exodus 15:1-3 Then Moses and the Israelites sang this song to the LORD:
"I will sing to the LORD, for he is highly exalted.
The horse and its rider he has hurled into the sea.
The LORD is my strength and my song; he has become my salvation.
He is my God, and I will praise him, my father's God, and I will exalt him.
The LORD is a warrior; the LORD is his name."

David led the people of Israel in abandoned praise when he brought the Ark of God's presence back to Israel.

2 Sam 6:14,15 David, wearing a linen ephod, danced before the LORD with all his might, while he and the entire house of Israel brought up the ark of the LORD with shouts and the sound of trumpets.

Both these examples indicate loud and energetic songs. They were really glad because God had saved them and was present with them!

When we understand that we have been saved for eternity by the blood of Jesus and moreover eternal life with Him starts now, there is a place for energetic praise and thanks as we sing! 'Western world' congregations are often not used to lively movement when they praise, but they can be gently encouraged to clap as they sing!

Intimacy

In recent years there has been a renewed understanding of the place of intimacy in our worship, thanks largely to the teaching of John Wimber and the Vineyard church that he founded. The Bible makes it clear that God is looking for an intimate relationship with the people He created. Right at the beginning God is seen walking in the Garden of Eden in the cool of the day looking for Adam to talk to. But Adam had already disobeyed God's command not to eat of the tree in the middle of the garden and so he was hiding.

The story of the Bible is how God has made it possible for that relationship of intimacy to be restored, by sending His only son Jesus for us. The intimate relationship that Jesus has with His Father in Heaven (and which He lived out on earth) is what He longs for us to have. He is the 'first born of many brothers' (Romans 8:29).

So Jesus commended for all time the actions of Mary of Bethany, when she sat at His feet, as close as she could get, listening to Him and 'watching His every move'.

Luke 10:41,42 "Martha, Martha," the Lord answered, "you are worried and upset about many things, but only one thing is needed. Mary has chosen what is better, and it will not be taken away from her."

At the end of the Bible John the Apostle shares his vision of the redeemed church-

Rev 21:2,3 I saw the Holy City, the new Jerusalem, coming down out of heaven from God, prepared as a bride beautifully dressed for her husband. And I heard a loud voice from the throne saying, "Now the dwelling of God is with men, and he will live with them. They will be his people, and God himself will be with them and be their God."

The use of the picture of bride and groom as well as the imagery of God living with people both point to the intimacy of relationship that God has in mind for us.

As we worship we should expect to experience God's nearness to us. Maybe it will be his reassuring presence, His voice in our inner ear or His healing touch. We need to teach worshippers to look out for the signs of God's presence and make space after worship to share any prophetic words or pictures that God may have given for the church - to give a testimony to something God has done - or for further prayer ministry.

Awe

God showed His awesome presence to the Israelites at Sinai when they had miraculously escaped from Egypt:

Ex 19:16-19 On the morning of the third day there was thunder and lightning, with a thick cloud over the mountain, and a very loud trumpet blast. Everyone in the camp trembled. Then Moses led the people out of the camp to meet with God, and they stood at the foot of the mountain. Mount Sinai was covered with smoke, because the LORD descended on it in fire. The smoke billowed up from it like smoke from a furnace, the whole mountain trembled violently, and the sound of the trumpet grew louder and louder.

People in the Old Testament who 'saw' God expected to die!

Ex 19:21 The LORD said to him, "Go down and warn the people so they do not force their way through to see the LORD and many of them perish."

The writer to the Hebrews points out that, although Jesus has brought us back into God's presence and we can come to Him with confidence, we should still take what He says seriously and remember that he is God Almighty:

Heb 12:18-25 You have not come to a mountain that can be touched and that is burning with fire; to darkness, gloom and storm; to a trumpet blast or to such a voice speaking words that those who heard it begged that no further word be spoken to them, because they could not bear what was commanded: "If even an animal touches the mountain, it must be stoned." The sight was so terrifying that Moses said, "I am trembling with fear." But you have come to Mount Zion, to the heavenly Jerusalem, the city of the living God. You have come to thousands upon thousands of angels in joyful assembly, to the church of the firstborn, whose names are written in heaven. You have come to God, the judge of all men, to the spirits of righteous men made perfect, to Jesus the mediator of a new covenant, and to the sprinkled blood that speaks a better word than the blood of Abel. See to it that you do not refuse him who speaks.

The worship at the throne of God, which we read about in Revelation, is truly awesome:

Rev 4:2-11 At once I was in the Spirit, and there before me was a throne in heaven with someone sitting on it. And the one who sat there had the appearance of jasper and carnelian. A rainbow, resembling an emerald, encircled the throne. ... From the throne came flashes of lightning, rumblings and peals of thunder. Before the throne, seven lamps were blazing. These are the seven spirits of God. ... Whenever the living creatures give glory, honour and thanks to him who sits on the throne and who lives for ever and ever, the twenty-four elders fall down before him who sits on the throne, and worship him who lives for ever and ever. They lay their crowns before the throne and say: "You are worthy, our Lord and God, to receive glory and honour and power,..."

If our worship here is a pale reflection of that in Heaven (a practice for eternity, if you like) we should expect our songs to reflect the awesome holiness of God. There should be a sense of the majestic in the music, sometimes a space for silence, - and it may be right to fall on our knees or faces before Him!

2 Values in Worship

God-centred songs

We value singing songs addressed directly to God rather than just about Him (and in the third person). Our songs are not primarily a teaching vehicle for the congregation. While we want unbelievers to be welcomed when we worship, the words of our songs are not addressed to them to draw them into faith. The words of our songs should remind us of whom God is in *all* His glory, majesty and power as well as His compassion, mercy and salvation. Our faith is increased as we sing about Him and then we are able to make a personal response.

Accessibility

Both the words and the music of our songs of worship need to be accessible and relevant to the experience and culture of the congregation and its milieu. We need to be wary of using too much obscure Biblical imagery in our lyrics (there is not usually the opportunity to explain it). The music of the song (rhythm, beat, melody, instruments used) needs to be in the cultural language understood by the present congregation, as well as the outsiders whom they are seeking to draw into the church.

Time

Coming to worship is like making a journey; we decide to do it, make a start, have in mind where we are going and encounter various things 'en route'.

In the Old Testament, Solomon dedicated the temple (2 Chron 5:2) by bringing in the ark (the presence of God), singing praises, praying and falling on his face in worship.(2 Chron 7:3). The wise men came on a long journey from the East to worship the infant Jesus like this and ended up bowing before Him (Matt 2:11). This all took a sustained period of time.

We recognise that we often need a period of uninterrupted singing in order to get to the place of reconsecration in the presence of God. Worship is a process that takes time; choosing several songs in a good order (see later) can help a worshipper to proceed into the presence of God.

No 'hype'

There is no need for the worship leader to 'whip up' the worshippers by exhorting them to praise more enthusiastically or by playing faster and louder! Someone has said 'We don't 'hype' the Holy Spirit up, He comes down'. By all means remind the worshippers that God loves them and is delighted with their worship.

Flexibility

Since it is the Holy Spirit who inspires true worship (John 4:23,24) He is the ultimate leader. We need to be flexible enough in our singing to follow His lead, and, if necessary, adapt what we had planned beforehand.

Sometimes in a time of worship it becomes clear that the worshippers are not yet ready to sing the song planned (e.g. a song of consecration, or one expressing intimacy). It is helpful if a worship leader can play a more appropriate song instead without disturbing the 'flow' of worship.

If there is a sense of God's holiness after the singing of a particular song, it may be appropriate to be silent rather than continue singing (2 Chron 5:14)

If the worship leader senses that people are being reminded of the needs of the world outside as they sing, it may be right to let the musicians play while the people are encouraged to speak out their prayers.

3 Introducing Renewed Worship in a Traditional Setting

Getting started

Changing the style of worship in a church is something that needs to be handled very carefully, as there is so much at stake. Many a church has come to grief over this issue. If there is to be an obvious change (for example, from the use of a robed choir to a band with microphones!) there is almost bound to be some opposition.

Most people feel insecure faced with change and become defensive. Some people, stressed by the 'rat-race' of working life, seek solace in church worship where they hope everything will stay the same and familiar.

Some are offended by any show of emotion in public, particularly in a church, and react negatively to singing lines like 'I love you' to God. Many people are frightened by the activity of the Holy Spirit, particularly when they don't understand it and no one has taken the time to explain it.

This all creates a difficult seedbed for renewed worship. However there will be some who are longing for something new and alive, who have begun to experience the power of the Holy Spirit in their personal lives, and are eager to express that in church worship.

One way forward

Start small and simple

It is much easier to start something new with a small group in a home setting, where people have come together to grow in their faith and are open to learning something new. This is also a much less exposed place for a new worship leader to 'learn the ropes'. A guitar, because it is so portable and is relatively easy to pick up the basic chord structures needed, is an ideal instrument to play to accompany worship. If there is no one in the group who can give a lead musically, use a tape or CD to accompany the singing. (e.g. The New Wine Acoustic Worship CD)

• Choose some simple songs, which focus on who God is and allow the believer to express a response of love and adoration.

• Encourage the group to learn the songs by repeating them so that they can sing them directly to the Lord.

• Allow time for people to relax into this so that they are open to the Lord ministering by His Holy Spirit in whatever way He chooses.

Usually, when a group enjoys worshipping together in this way, someone will want to learn to play an instrument, maybe a guitar. The younger the person, the more time they have to practice and improve!

Growing a worshipping community

When 2 or 3 groups have become used to worshipping in this way, it may be possible to meet together as a larger group for a monthly meeting in church - after the evening service, for example.

• Use the worship leaders from the individual groups to lead the singing in the same way.

• Ideally one should lead, playing the guitar and singing, while the others sing echoes or harmony and play, maybe keyboard and percussion for rhythm.

As this larger group gathers to worship and knows the Lord's presence, others will want to join. As the group increases in size, the worship leaders' experience will grow and they will possibly want to add a couple more instruments for variety. When numbers are sufficient to warrant greater volume, the time has come to consider adding a sound system - (and finding someone with the skill to run it!)

How do we find people to play in a band? - No one plays an instrument in our church!

You may think you know everyone in your church, but its surprising what gifts people will hide from you! God promises to supply all our needs (Phil 4:19). The best way to get instrumental players and vocalists is to pray for them and then wait to see whom God will provide. By all means make it known that you are looking and praying for a bass player or drummer etc, as well. Those who profess to have very little skill sometimes just lack confidence - give them a try and they will often 'come up trumps'! (The same is true vice versa - namely; those who push themselves forward as 'the best' often have a somewhat overrated view of their ability).

If you do not do auditions, (and they can be rather threatening!) offer a new player a place in the band for one Sunday - maybe as a fill-in for someone who is away. That way you can see how things turn out and whether you would want to offer anything further or just thank them for stepping in on this occasion.

Maintaining unity

As the worshipping community grows there is an excitement that God is 'on the move' but there are also more opportunities for dissension and disagreement and we need to guard our unity. The arena of worship is so crucial to the life and health of a church that it is often the most under attack from Satan.

Eph 4:3 Make every effort to keep the unity of the Spirit through the bond of peace

The relationship most open to attack is the one between the church leader and the worship leader. The church leader (vicar, minister, pastor) is responsible before God for the church and needs to know that he has the support and co-operation of the worship leader. The worship leader therefore needs to understand the vision of the vicar for the church and be able to follow and work for it. The worship leader who cannot take direction from his leader is likely to create dissension.

The church leader needs to take time to cultivate a good relationship with his worship leader, to share his heart for the work of God in the community, to encourage him personally and see that he is not over-loaded. (Most worship leaders in our churches are holding down full-time jobs in the community as well as caring for their families and taking the responsibility for the running of the worship.)

Maintaining a healthy structure

• The church leader needs to build a good relationship with his worship leader; training, encouraging and thanking him.

• The worship leader needs to care for his band members in the same way.

Rom15:5,6 May the God who gives endurance and encouragement give you a spirit of unity among yourselves as you follow Christ Jesus, so that with one heart and mouth you may glorify the God and Father of our Lord Jesus Christ.

How to do it

• Clear communication is important. Clarify who is responsible for what, how long the 'worship time' is expected to last, who chooses the songs etc. This avoids needless misunderstandings and hurt feelings.

• Be friends with one another. Spend time having fun and getting to know each other as people.

• Pray together, not only for the worship but also for the personal needs of each other and families.

• Share vision together. It is probably helpful to go off to a conference on worship and reflect together on what you have learnt and can put into practice in your church.

• Be open with each other, particularly when someone has been offended, and be forgiving. Don't let resentment build.

4 The Worship Leader

A worship leader's main task is to enable the church to worship. As such they are a servant-leader of the church. Finding the right worship leader is key to the development of renewed worship. The most musically gifted member of the church (or home group) may not necessarily be that person (although musical skill is obviously a qualification - see later).

Qualifications

The following list of qualifications are suggested in order of priority:

- A worshipper. A leader must be born-again and developing a personal worship life of their own, in private as well as in public. A worship leader cannot lead the people of God somewhere they have never been. A worshipper would be turning up for the meetings of the church whether they were taking a leading role or not.

- A 'servant leader' of the congregation. A worship leader is not a performer but aims to help the congregation to minister to God as they worship. This means singing the songs that enable them to do this, rather than any personal esoteric choice. It means not blaming the congregation for not getting 'involved' in worship but encouraging them. It is shown in their love for people in kind and courteous dealings with them (even if they are being critical! see Chapter 11).

- A good relationship with the overall church leader. Someone who understands, like the centurion of old (Matt 8:5), that they are under authority, will work with the vision of the church rather than building a platform for their own talents. When the church leader and the worship leader are friends, the church can grow, whatever the outward spirituality (high church, evangelical, charismatic) of that church.

- A good reputation among the people. We are not looking for 'sainthood' here (!) but the church will follow the lead of someone whom they respect. Conversely, someone who is known to lose their temper, or drink too much, or have a sexual relationship outside marriage, or be dating someone who is patently not a believer will not inspire the right sort of followers. This does not mean that we should hide all difficulties, but rather be seen to be bringing them under the Lordship of Christ, by being accountable, getting prayer counselling where appropriate and being humble and repentant.

Skills

• Musical skill. The level of skill will depend on the size of the worshipping group. But a worship leader needs to be able to project a singing voice in tune and preferably play an accompanying instrument adequately so as not to be a distraction! As the group grows the leader should give time and energy to improving their skill (Psalm 33:3) through day workshops, books and CD's, lessons etc.

• Ability to lead a band. This means being able to inspire a band to play well, to worship together, pray together and be united. It means understanding what instruments will produce a pleasing sound together (not everyone who volunteers will be able to play in the same band at the same time), as well as producing the sound. In rehearsal, a wise worship leader listens to the suggestions of members of the band, acknowledges where they are good and implements them where appropriate.

• Ability to 'spot' giftings in potential band players and train them.

• Ability and desire to train up other worship leaders and release other bands with them.

Character

• Humble. Someone who is wanting to serve the Lord and His church, rather than have a 'trip' by performing. This might mean being willing to lead a small and relatively insignificant group in worship when asked.

• Teachable. Someone who is still willing to learn from those who are more experienced, and who can take direction from the church leader, will continue to develop and improve. The 'ready-made maestro' may have more difficulty fitting in to the church family. Someone who has led worship in a previous church needs to have time worshipping as a member of a new congregation so that they become fully part of the new 'family' with its particular values and ways. It may be quite important to talk about what the church's aim in worship is so that there are no misunderstandings. The new worship leader needs to know to whom they are accountable so that they can check out how they are doing.

• Reliable. Turning up on time for practices and worship meetings is vital for a leader.

• Available. Someone who can commit to being there every Sunday or as often as needed, is going to be more useful as a worship leader than someone who is always away on business, visiting relatives or 'sick'. Often professional musicians have to work at the weekend and so they do not make good leaders of Sunday worship.

5 The Band

When a new and contemporary worship style is established in a church and the numbers in the congregation are growing, it will be an advantage to have a band accompany the worship. Initially this will help with the volume (one voice and an acoustic guitar can lead up to 50 people) but it will also greatly enhance the style and variety of worship. Boosting the rhythm section by adding drums and/or percussion helps the celebration element. Using a keyboard to add bass and treble notes and/or help carry the tune, will aid learning new songs. Adding a flute or a violin or cello to play incidentally, will enhance songs of intimacy.

A basic band needs:

Tune:	lead vocal, or other vocalists
Rhythm:	guitar, drums, percussion
Sound:	Bass - bass guitar, double bass, keyboard
	Midrange - guitar, keyboard, male voice
	Treble - female voice, electric guitar, flute

Some of these instruments rely on a sound system to produce sound (bass guitar, electric guitar, electric keyboard). A drum-kit, while not requiring a sound system itself, needs to be played very sensitively (brushes only?) if there is no PA. In this instance, congas would be a better option. The musicians (particularly the keyboard player) need to know what they are contributing to the overall sound so that they produce depth, colour and richness.

Most musicians do not need to play all the time, (the worship leader and their instrument might be an exception here). In fact they need to develop an ear for when their instrument is really needed. (See chapter 9) This is particularly true for 'incidental' instruments such as flutes, violins, electric guitar, trumpet, cymbals, vocal harmony lines etc. Played at the right time these instruments can help to usher in the presence of God. Played incessantly throughout worship they can become plain irritating!

It is often preferable to start a band with a basic line-up of: lead vocal, guitar, bass, drums and keyboard. Get used to playing together before you add extra instruments. It is easier to get a decent sound with fewer instruments. Many churches make the mistake of using everyone who volunteers and wonder why the sound is indistinct or 'muddy'. In the case of more musicians being available, train up a new band and rota them to lead worship.

What am I looking for in a band member?

Qualifications

1) Servant-heart. A band member should want to help (rather than perform) and to bring glory to God. You find this servant-heart in people who are still prepared to play even when it doesn't suit their social diary!

2) Accountable to the worship leader. A band member needs to listen to what the worship leader wants from them with regard to the music, as well as with regard to dress and behaviour in the band.

3) Available. The best musical technique in the world is worth little if a band member is unavailable for the practices and the services.

Skills

1) Adequate musicality on the instrument. If you want to be flexible in your worship style and value musicians who can play extemporarily, you don't need to ask them necessarily what grade they have reached. Try them out. Trained musicians on the other hand may take some time to learn how to be less tied to the sheet music. Expect to improve on your instrument by practising and taking lessons where necessary.

2) Team-player not a soloist. A band member needs to listen to others playing and learn to blend. Sometimes he will need to stop playing to let another instrument shine. This is not about impressing the crowd!

3) Punctuality. The player who consistently turns up late for rehearsal and services, holds up the progress of the whole band. Any sound-checks are rendered difficult.

Character

1) Humble. A band member needs to hear the leader say 'Do play here and don't play there'. He may need to let someone else play for the 'big' service.

2) Open and honest. Friends in the congregation will know his faults; its best to keep short accounts with the Lord. Friends also take advantage of familiarity to criticise the band; a band member needs to be able to handle it appropriately - (maybe take it to the leader).

3) Teachable. Both on the instrument and in their walk with the Lord.

4) No ill-feeling with other band members. If it arises, face it and deal with it. Openness and forgiveness are the key.

6 Church Leadership and the Musical Director

David Pytches

Bishop David Pytches founded the New Wine conferences from which Soul Survivor grew. He was also for many years vicar of St. Andrews church, Chorleywood. His own experience of leading a large and growing church and managing the changes involved is reflected in the following chapter:

Changes

'Vicar wants Rock Group in Church - Out goes the old - in comes the new'

Local newspaper headlines reporting changes at St.Nicholas, Durham, when George Carey (now the Archbishop of Canterbury) was the rector, according to his book *'The Church in the Market Place'*.

Any changes are threatening. Church leaders inevitably think twice before embarking on any new ventures. No church leader likes upsetting his congregation. Church leaders contemplating making a change might profitably read a book on the subject before seeking to negotiate a major change in the life of any Church. The following areas will be matters of special concern to the leader wanting to change the ethos / style of the worship in the local church.

The leader is the leader

It is important that everybody understands that in the final analysis the church leader has the last word about the worship in church; the normal time allowed for worship in song, the choice of songs, the words, the tunes and the doctrine expressed. Obviously for a major change they will consult the appropriate people - PCC etc.

Selecting a song worship leader

The whole process of appointing a song worship leader needs to be soaked in prayer. It is so important to get it right.

What kind of person is required?

Obviously a truly born again Christian with a passion for Jesus and open to the Holy Spirit. Humility and a loyal submissive attitude to the church leadership are essential. This is basically a servant ministry and we do not want anyone with his or her own platform agenda.

There is something indefinable about a good worship leader - it's called the *anointing*.

Preferably someone who has experience as a regular worshipper, if not worship leader, in a charismatic congregation. Its probably best to have someone under thirty for this kind of worship but not essential - but this will depend upon the kind of congregation. Gender is not an issue in such an appointment.

Full time or part time?

If full time, the church leader will need to consult the church council or trustees about sufficient funding. I made suggestions and asked the church treasurer to work out details of a salary and any other expenses that might be involved - this may include buying or renting accommodation.

It is the leader's responsibility to see that this is done and that the worship leader appointed knows who to speak to about their finances. If a person has to travel for an interview its proper for them to be reimbursed for travelling expenses.

If they have to do the job voluntarily they will probably have to be part time and earning a living in secular employment.

How does the church leader find the person required for the job?

There are several simple options:

a) The first place to look is within the congregation. Is there anyone there who might be suitable? Encourage such a person to attend a New Wine or Soul Survivor training day or weekend. *(Most of the best worship leaders in our generation have grown this way, because they have already imbibed the vision of the church and have a good relationship with the church leader. Ed.)*

b) Ask around, for example in the New Wine network.

c) Consult the leadership of other churches which already have the style of worship wanted for the congregation. Where another church has a good song worship leader there will probably be quite a few other aspirants waiting in the wings.

d) Recommendations from others.

e) Advertising. It is important, if this is done, to let applicants know as soon as possible if they have been short listed or not. Potential candidates get very frustrated being left in the dark and it's gracious to inform them of their position as soon as possible.

It is vital to have references if the applicant is unknown to the church leader - not just from friends but others; eg. the church leader where the applicant is currently worshipping and their current employer. If the applicant is not working, the question is 'why not?' It is helpful to speak to the referees on the phone.

It's good to include others on the interviewing panel - both male and female selectors. If this is a completely new step for the congregation then it may be good to have a leader from another 'charismatic' church to help in some areas of discernment - such as gifting, anointing etc.

Length of the appointment

If the applicant is previously unknown, or unproven in directing music in worship, the initial period of appointment needs to be as tentative as possible. A short term contract can be made, to be reviewed after a few months and then a year's contract might be helpful. It is important to avoid being settled with a director of music before one is really sure you have the right person. It is also important to ensure that all normal legal obligations with regard to employment are met. This is especially true if the person needs to move to take up the appointment.

Questions about the Job Description

If the church leader is not sure about what he wants the person to do, it might help to get one or two job descriptions from others who are already employing a song worship leader.

a) Are they to be the *overall* director responsible for finding an organist required for a funeral or wedding or even a traditional hymn in the main service?

b) Will they be expected to make these arrangement etc, or is there some other overall director under whom the person being appointed is expected to work?

c) What about their relationship with the choir leader for special events - carol services etc? These things will need to be clarified from the start. (*In our experience, it is almost impossible to find a good worship leader who can play and arrange traditional church music as well as being 'on the cutting edge' of new worship. Most will have a preference and ability in one direction or the other but not both equally. Ed.*)

d) Is the music director expected to delegate to others and to train up new song worship leaders for different groups in the church - home groups, new church plants etc and even as stand-ins for the song worship leader themselves?

e) Are they responsible for finding volunteers and arranging a rota for operators of the p.a. system? If not, clarify who has that responsibility.

f) Is the musical director expected to keep a file of words and music for future occasions - if so where?

g) Are they expected to make the new acetates, or to oversee song projection? If so, how? Will there be any help from the church office for this?

h) Will they be responsible for finding volunteers and arranging operators for the overhead projector or is that someone else's duty?

Relationship between worship leader and church leader

Leading worship together

During worship it is important for the worship leader and the church leader to be in eye-contact. Because, so often, a time of open worship inspires the use of the gifts of the Spirit - like tongues or prophecy etc - I always had an arrangement with the person directing the worship in song that I would take over when that occurred - and would give them a signal when, or if, they should start up again.

Weekly meetings

I met each week with my song worship leader. I wanted to avoid songs that were too wordy; had bad grammar, poor poetry, didn't scan and above all might be unscriptural. I also wanted to ensure a proper focus on Christ Jesus and him crucified.

We discussed together the way things were going, the composition of the group and the balance of the songs to be included in the worship. Some might be omitted when the time came. This was to ensure that the worship songs had a good range, could include any that fitted in with the day or the address, and did not include too many new ones - especially those of the worship leader, though I think the writing of home grown songs needs encouraging.

There may come a time when such a clear understanding between the church leader and the song leader exists that these meetings can be less frequent.

Complaints and criticisms

Because the Church leader has the final responsibility they will also receive occasional complaints from the congregation. Those who complain are usually trying to help but don't always express themselves tactfully and these seem to come over as criticisms. The leader will evaluate any they get before sharing them with the musical director. Criticisms need to be mixed with plenty of encouragement. Song worship leaders tend to be extra sensitive which is what makes them so good at sensing how the Spirit is leading in times of worship.

Back-up and support

As a church leader I always urged our PCC to bend over backwards to help all those holding leadership positions in the church, and to respond as positively as possible in helping them get all the equipment they felt necessary. (e.g. PA) They were doing the job on our behalf. This was especially the case with youth leaders, Sunday school leaders and worship leaders.

The question of copyright

The list of songs actually sung needs to be kept for copyright purposes. As soon as any church begins to introduce new music for worship and to reproduce words on an overhead projector, closed circuit TV or in an expanded songbook the matter of copyright arises. In Britain any original material is automatically the copyright of the author, composer or publisher whether the music is registered or not. Those who produced the music are entitled to a fee. Many song writers, composers and publishers give themselves to this ministry full time and need their fees (just as professional people like solicitors or veterinary surgeons would do) to maintain themselves and their families financially.

I say this because some shrug off their obligation to pay fees by claiming that since the songs were inspired by God, Christians should not expect to be paid for them. All churches, however, are morally obliged to pay up. Alternatively their musicians can start writing their own songs!

The organisation to contact about this is: Christian Copyright Licensing (Europe) Ltd, PO Box 1339, Eastbourne, East Sussex, BN2I 1AD.
Telephone: 01323 417711 Fax: 01323 417722 Email: info@ccli.co.uk
Website: www.ccli.co.uk

7 Leading Worship

Neil Bennetts

Neil Bennetts leads worship at New Wine conferences as well as leading worship at his home church at Holy Trinity, Cheltenham, where he is on the staff with overall responsibility for the development of the worship. Here he offers some guidelines for leading worship, which he has culled from his experience of leading in a small group in the home, as well as in the larger setting of the church or big gathering:

Centrality of worship

Worship, I believe, is central to the life and ministry of the church, whether in teaching or preaching, in junior church, in prayer and intercession, in evangelism and discipleship. In many ways, it is the wellspring from which all else takes place.

This means that a worship leader may find himself leading worship in many different situations. Looking back over the last few years, I have led worship in cell groups, at Sunday services, at Alpha meetings, at prayer meetings, for conferences and celebrations. I have led worship at 7.00 in the morning, before lunch, after lunch, in the evening, and into the night. Worship is central to our vision. But whatever the situation you find yourself leading worship in, many of the issues are the same.

The worship leader

In Chronicles, we see it was the Levites who were responsible for leading the worship. Levites were priests. Leading worship was a priestly function. Under the New Covenant, through the death of Jesus, we are all priests. We are all involved in the act of worship.

> 1 Cor 14:26 *When you come together, everyone has a hymn, or a word of instruction, a revelation, a tongue or an interpretation.*

In a congregation, actually managing this process is not necessarily straightforward.

It is only comparatively recently (in the last half of the 20th century), that our, now common, understanding of a worship leader, has come about. In the past, this role may have been shared jointly between a pastor and organist, or it may have been a role undertaken corporately by the fellowship (Acts 2 may imply this was the case in the early church). In the future the leadership of worship may have to develop into different forms. But for now, this current typical role is the one I want to focus on.

The primary function of the worship leader

Worship leading is primarily an enabling role: enabling the gathered people of God to worship God and bring acceptable sacrifices to him. David Pytches says that a great worship leader 'recognises that he is not there to minister to the people but to enable them to minister to God'.

My failure as a worship leader comes primarily, not because I fluff chords, or sing out of tune, or get the words wrong, but when I don't allow people to engage with God.

Calling

I believe that, as in any area of Christian ministry, God calls people to lead worship. So we should make every effort to understand God's call on our life for this ministry. The Levites were 'chosen and designated by name to give thanks to the Lord'. (1Chron 16:41). There was no accident about their involvement.

Under authority

I believe that for a worship leader to be able to operate effectively, they need to be fully integrated within the leadership of the local church. They need to have hands laid on them for the task of leading worship. They need to be publicly recognised by the church leadership in their role. They need to recognise that, as part of the leadership, they are accountable to the overall leader of the church. The three worship leaders described in Chronicles (Asaph, Jeduthun and Heman) themselves were 'under the supervision of the King'. (1 Chron 25:6)

One of the main sources of strength for my ministry has been the relationship I have had with my church leader (Mark Bailey) and the whole church leadership team and staff at Trinity Church, Cheltenham. They have been such strong supporters. They remain loyal to me, pray for me, guide me and encourage me when I feel I have made mistakes. In many ways I have worked out my calling with them.

A relationship of trust

For the whole church to move deeper in expressions of worship, there needs to be a relationship of trust between the worship leader and the congregation. Where the congregation trusts its worship leader they are likely to be open to change, to follow where you lead.

We have already looked at the need for worship leaders to serve the leadership of the church. This in itself helps the congregation trust the worship leader. When I lead worship in Trinity Church, people know I am directly responsible to Mark, the vicar, for what I do.

Your congregation needs to know that you are there to serve, not to fulfil your own agenda, to further your own ministry, or provide a platform for your own development, but to help them worship. They need to feel that you act with integrity - the way that you live your life off 'stage' reflecting your role on 'stage'.

Losing the trust of the congregation

This trust can be broken if, for example, you choose material that they don't find helpful, or play in a style that they can't relate to. It may be broken if you try and move things too quickly.

Unfortunately, trust lost is trust hard to get back. Congregations will remember the time that you led those heavy electric rock songs during communion. They will remember the time you sang your 'new song' for 20 minutes without stopping. They will remember the time you didn't get the hint when the entire church was seated, reading papers and drinking the after service coffee whilst you pursued doggedly on with your worship set for the full hour and a half!

I value the trust I have with our congregation and protect it vigorously. As new worship leaders come up through our church, I spend time working with them, helping with their song choice, organisation and worship leading style. The reason for this is, not to be overly controlling, but to help them develop a relationship of trust with the congregation.

A sacrifice of worship

For all worshippers there is a cost to true worship. This is especially true for worship leaders. As David said 'I will not sacrifice to the Lord my God burnt offerings that cost me nothing'. (2 Sam 24:24)

This often means that there is something of a sacrifice involved in leading worship. You may need to choose songs, arrange songs, even sing songs in such away that you may not ideally want to, for the sake of ensuring your congregation are able to worship God for themselves.

These might be some of the sacrifices that we face as worship leaders:

1. Time sacrifice. Time choosing songs, time rehearsing, getting to the church early and leaving late.

2. Financial sacrifice. It is difficult to get a really good sound out of a very cheap instrument. There may be sacrifices you have to make to ensure your instrument is adequate for the purpose.

3. For some, the amount of time and energy required may mean that you can't pursue your career in the same way. You may have to decline promotions, especially if they mean moving around the country.

4. Image. Standing in front of a church with a guitar singing love songs to God is, to many people, not the most 'cool' thing - especially to work colleagues.

Prominence and invisibility

The impact that worship leaders can have on the life of the church can be immense. Invariably in our churches and congregations today, the worship leader is one of the most prominent people in the church. The acoustics of the church and the need to be able to communicate with both congregation and band means that in most circumstances the worship leader will be both visible and audible to the congregation.

• Think about how you present yourself and the band - your clothing, your positioning as a group, or even how physically you may move about at the front of the church.

• Think about your vocal technique. Make sure the melody line is heard. Unnecessary embellishments could distract people.

• Try and keep intervention to a minimum. Long wordy explanations in between each song are likely to move people's attention off God and back to you. In fact I hardly ever say anything now when I lead worship. Occasionally I may pray, or say something right at the beginning or the end, but normally I say nothing.

• Prophetic / new songs can enrich worship. Some congregations will be ready and open and find it more helpful than others. If the congregation cannot participate, then their ability to worship God and minister to Him may be lessened.

Worship as a journey towards intimacy

One of the words used for worship in the Bible means 'to draw near to kiss'. There is a sense that every time we come to worship as the gathered church, we embark on a journey towards an intimate encounter with our Father in heaven. This may mean different things at different times. It may be a sense of God's unconditional love. It may be a time where we are abandoned in extravagant praise and thanksgiving for God's character and intervention in our lives. It may be a time when we plead with God for our nation. It may be a time where we are lost in wonder at Jesus' death for us on the cross.

Preparing a smooth journey

I have usually found that congregations like this journey to be smooth. As a worship leader, you not only need to sense the Lord's leading for a particular time of worship, you also need to manage the way you get there. This means that as we move from song to song in our worship, we need to think about that journey. The journey can be made smooth with a logical progression in the theme or intent of each song. For example, it probably doesn't help to have a song about revival, followed by a song about being in the arms of God, followed by a song about spiritual warfare. The congregation may feel that things are getting a bit bumpy.

I am not one to encourage no preparation before a service. In fact I strongly recommend it. But I would also encourage worship leaders to be responsive to what they sense God doing during the worship.

How to prepare to be flexible!

- Take time to develop a repertoire of songs that you feel comfortable playing. If you work with a band regularly, work at developing a repertoire of songs that you all know.

- Learn songs, and get your band to learn songs so that the unavailability of the music right in front of them is not a constraint. The sight of 5 band members all searching through files in the middle of a time of worship can put people off.

- In your preparation, maybe make a list of more songs than you will need, but which could allow you to move in different directions during the time of worship if needed.

- Keep your eyes open now and then. Look at the people as they worship. Do they look as if they are engaging with God?

- Work closely with your leaders. I have often found that those leading our services can be more sensitive to what God is doing in the worship than I am. Let them come to the front and lead the church in tongues or intercession, for example.

- Don't be afraid to stop. Sometimes, God may want other things than the songs you have prepared.

- Understand how God speaks to you best during these times. We are all different, and the way that God speaks to us is unique.

- Don't be afraid of making mistakes. Learn from them afterwards!

A unique experience - every time.

Every time we worship God we enter into a unique experience, never to be repeated. We need to remember that we come to worship a living, life breathing, awesome God. He is the same yesterday today and for evermore, but everyday he reveals more of himself to us, more of his character, more of his beauty, more of his love.

I am constantly surprised by God's intervention in our worship. We may be singing a very familiar song, in a small group on a weekday night. But in those moments God inhabits his peoples' praise, speaks his truth and healing and favour into our lives. I need to remember this every time I lead worship. What an awesome and exciting thing.

8 Choosing The Right Songs

The journey

Understanding that a time of worship is like a journey with a beginning, a middle and an end will help in song selection. The Old Testament worshippers going to the temple enacted the progress from the outer courts (thanksgiving and praise), through the inner courts (cleansing and sanctification), into the sanctuary (God's holy presence).

The beginning:

We need to start where the people are. Often people are tired and weary from the work of the week. They need to be reminded of the truth of who God is: how great He is, His love and mercy, His past acts. Songs declaring the truth and that are easy to sing and/or familiar are good here. It is usually a mistake to start with a new song because harassed people are in no mood to learn songs! Songs of invitation to worship are also good to open with. 'Come, now is the time to worship.'

The end:

We need to know where we are taking people. The general aim is to experience the presence of God. Pray as you choose songs that God would show you a particular goal for this worship session:

- The throne room of heaven, sense of God's holy awesomeness.
- The presence of the Father God and his unconditional love.
- The foot of the cross, brokenness and rededication.
- The place of intimacy where God speaks.
- Intercession for the needs of others.

All these might be possibilities, but any one may be experienced by different worshippers in one worship time. Take advice from the service leader or preacher, they may have a particular theme in mind.

The middle:

Choose songs that follow a 'flow' both in words and music. Although you may use a number of songs in one worship time, the whole should be as one song of worship offered up to the Lord

Creating a 'flow'

Analyse your songs

A song is made up of words, tune, rhythm and tempo:

Words: Praise. Thanks. Adoration. Love. Repentance. Awe. Intercession. Consecration.

Tune: Catchy, Complex. Well-known, unknown. High, low. Memorable chorus.

Rhythm: Strong. Lilting. Syncopated. Straightforward.

Tempo: Fast, slow. Moderate. Flexible.

Some songs have many words, some are simple. A good worship set has a mixture. Too many wordy songs become too heavy and the focus drifts.

Hymns: There are many wonderful old hymns that have stood the test of time. They were themselves often written in a time of revival and the truths they convey are still fresh. The right hymn in the middle of a worship set can 'lift the roof'. Since many hymn tunes were not written to be sung to a strong beat, a contemporary band will have to work hard at accompanying them. Try to keep to the same tune but work at the rhythm. Some hymns will be easier than others. We have sometimes used the organ alongside the band (the organ has to be in the same pitch as the band!) The swell of the organ sound can lift the spirits of the congregation. The use of a hymn and the incorporation of the organ can often help in the transition from traditional worship to a more contemporary style.

Simple songs: Where a worshipping group does not have access to printed words (e.g. in a home group setting), you will need to choose simple songs if you don't want to be singing a solo! Another idea here is to use the choruses from songs which are usually well-known - (you could always have one person with the words singing the verses in between).

Follow a theme in the words.

Pick up a line or phrase in one song and let it find an echo in the next one. Avoid jumping from a song of intercession into celebration, then intimacy and back to intercession.

A good plan:

• Start with a song declaring the truth about God (this reminds the people who they have come to worship).

• You could follow this with a song of thanks (they have now remembered that He is good!).

• Then a song that is personal to the believer (He is good to me!).

• A song which expresses the believer's response of love and adoration to God.

• Then a song of reconsecration (I give myself to You again).

You can follow this plan linking it to different themes such as the cross, God's mercy, God's love for the nations etc.

Create a musical flow.

• Consider the rhythm and tempo and avoid moving from fast to slow and back to fast. At the end of an upbeat song you may be able to repeat a chorus reflectively and more slowly in order to lead into a meditative song.

• Practice the band continuing to play at the end of a song, and moving seamlessly into the next song. Work out chord sequences and any key changes.

• If you think that a song will lead naturally into a time of open worship prepare the band for it (worship using it in the practice). Unless the congregation are very accustomed to singing in tongues, the band should try to keep to playing on the one final chord of the song.

• If a song leads into a time of intercession, likewise stick to a simple chord sequence at the end of the song, maybe just the 2 chords; keep the musicians playing and let the leader intercede from a microphone and encourage the people to pray out loud too, if that is appropriate. At the end of a time of prayer you can repeat the chorus of the song to gather all the people together again.

• After such a free time of worship or prayer the worship leader needs to discern what sort of song to lead into next - if there is to be one. Lead the people gently out of a time of quiet singing in tongues (an upbeat drum-based intro into a celebration song would probably be inappropriate here!).

New songs

Introduce one or, at the most, two per session. Some will be catchy and easily learnt, others more difficult (then only one a session!). Consider playing them as people are arriving for the service, or while communion is being distributed, so that they are being heard already. Spend time on these in practice.

A tired group will worship more readily using familiar songs. Be prepared to ditch a new song if it will distract the focus from God (even if you did spend the whole worship practice perfecting it!).

Favourite songs

Yours and the church's may not be the same! You are not there to play your favourite songs, but as a servant to the church to lead them into the Lord's presence. Gage when a 'hot favourite' has had its time with your group and needs to be rested.

Know your time limitations

Have a finishing time in mind. This will give you some idea as to how many songs to prepare. Have some other songs 'to hand', in case you need to alter direction, or get the 'nod' to extend the time.

Prepare the first half of your set tightly and the second half lightly.

Keep an eye on the clock and the church leader!

9 Using the Band to Best Effect

Ed Pask

Ed Pask with his band has led worship at New Wine conferences. Ed leads worship at his church, St, Paul's, Ealing.
God deserves to be given the best we have got and not something slipshod or second-rate. So worship leaders who have to lead a band and run a band practice will find his article invaluable:

Understanding how the different elements of a band fit together is vital in using the people you have to best effect. Having vision for what your musicians need to aim for is crucial to achieve a higher degree of professionalism in terms of musicianship and release a greater freedom of expression in worship. The basic premise behind the worship band is that of synergy, or 'the whole is greater than the sum of the parts'. Not only do we have a group of musicians who play together to add their sounds but the overall effect is one where the different types of sound complement one another and blend together to produce the most amazing 'picture'.

It is important to understand how the band is made up and what each person's role is if we are to make the transition from simply 'the sum of the parts' to an even bigger 'whole'. It is important too to understand which instrumental elements to put together in forming a band. In church worship bands we find ourselves putting together those that the Lord sends us, which can often be an interesting and unusual mix of instruments. Using the raw skills in the people we have as creatively as possible is the key to enabling amazing worship. In a typical worship band there are a number of key 'categories' of instruments, which we shall now look at in more detail.

The Band Structure

People are typically grouped together according to their function. Usually they are physically arranged so that people in the same group are near one another. This simply aids better communication. In the band there are likely to be elements of the following:

Harmonic instruments - laying out the chordal structure and development (of which one is likely to be the lead instrument, usually acoustic guitar or keyboard).

Acoustic Guitar, Keyboard, Mandolin, Electric Guitar (when playing rhythm guitar).

Rhythmic instruments - setting out the musical foundations and maintaining tempo.

Drums, Bass Guitar (this may be a surprise to some), Percussion.

Melodic instruments - developing a melody (usually solos, intros, fills, links etc).

Woodwind - flute, oboe, clarinet, Irish whistle, saxophone etc. Strings - violin, cello etc. Brass - trumpet, flugel horn etc (note: a brass section often includes saxes). Electric guitar (when playing lead or solo parts)

Vocals -

Lead (effectively the worship leader), Harmonist, Extemporist (improviser)

Note that some instruments can fall into several categories depending upon what they are doing, e.g. keyboard could be harmonic or melodic, or an acoustic guitar can fulfil a harmonic and a rhythmic role.

A more detailed description of what each instrument does and some pitfalls to avoid are described in section 3. But first, let's take a look at Three Golden Rules that provide a framework in which to play and help make the transition from 'the sum of the parts' to a greater 'whole'.

Three Golden Rules for a good sound

1. Create space

If you ever get to look at the score of a piece of orchestral music you'll notice that there is a complex sense of interplay between the instruments. It's almost as if a relay race is taking place where one instrument passes on the 'baton' of the tune to another. The variety of the sounds makes its impact because each voicing appears for a little while and holds the listener's interest before another takes over. If every instrument and voice were playing continuously nothing would stand out above the rest and the overall effect is an uninteresting and dull mush.

• Start by listening to each other. Think, 'how does what I'm doing fit in with everyone else?'

• Understand where the song or set is going - when are the times to add more or pull back?

• Start with nothing and add sounds to achieve the desired effect - remember, 'less is more':

Find the musical space to play in - where are the gaps?

Consider playing nothing, or playing very sparsely.

This requires discipline, as we all want to play our bit.

• Create basic arrangements - sometimes a thought-out 'score' is required to convey the desired structure. Don't be too prescriptive or you'll lose flexibility and spontaneity.

2. Play in strict tempo

The difference between an amateur sound and a professional one is more down to tight timing than fancy playing. A band that plays together conveys confidence to the congregation, which is essential if they are to feel relaxed under your leadership. Encourage each member of the band to 'feel' the rhythm, almost as if they had a metronome ticking away inside them. Melodic and harmonic instruments will need to do this the most, as they will be the least rhythmically grounded.

• Ideally, everyone should follow the drummer for their tempo. Listen out for the bright sounds which carry best, like the high hat or snare drum. But if the drummer is inexperienced and not very consistent then get people to follow the lead instrument instead.

• Songs (especially lively ones) tend to speed up as they go through. This usually happens little by little each time the song gets louder, e.g. between verse and chorus. Consciously try to slow down as you go into a louder passage and this should help cancel out the effect.

• Watch keyboards - they tend to be very loose at timing. This is because they are not primary rhythm instruments rather than because they are just sloppy!

• Don't become too rigid (and play by a metronome). Some elasticity is needed.

3. Give melodic instruments focus

A hallmark of amateurism is to have a flute or violin tootling away in the background throughout. It will either lose its impact, as it is ever-present, or it will grate on people's nerves. However, if a melodic instrument is heard from time to time, especially where there is a break in the singing, it has a very powerful effect. Encourage these instruments to look for the spaces and play into them

• Don't let them play all the time - 'less is more'.

• Discourage playing the tune. The voices will be doing this and in all likelihood the two won't quite be synchronised and will sound messy. Instead, encourage counter melody.

- Make the most of: introductions, links, fills (between chorus and verse).
- Improvising during open worship - simple is fine.
- Beware of brass instruments as they can be overpowering. Very careful planning is needed, e.g. tight fanfares and riffs are fantastic if they are played tightly.

Roles & Guidelines

The key to a smoothly functioning band is people knowing what they are supposed to be doing. This can simply come through lots of experience or can be learned surprisingly quickly if people understand their roles and have vision for what they are aiming for. Here are some thoughts of what each instrument should be aiming for. The list isn't exhaustive but should give guidelines. Try to add other instruments into the categories given.

Keyboard

The keyboard is the backbone of a worship band. It provides wonderful harmonic and melodic structure, adding colour to the chords that most guitarists don't have enough fingers for! It can also provide textures through voicings that 'fatten' the overall sound. Most keyboard players who offer their services in churches are pianists by background. Whilst the essence of the instruments are the same the application is very different. Armed with an understanding of the role of the keyboard in the band, a few weeks of practice should produce some impressive results that are an important step in the direction of excellence. Depending upon whether the keyboard is leading or supporting, in which case they may be more or less dominant, the following are some general guidelines for effective playing:

- Don't play the piano score from the music books as they are usually written to cover the whole spectrum of sound and so you will fill other people's space.
- Don't play the tune - leave it to the vocalists
- Go easy on the left hand parts - as it will tread on the bassist's toes

'So what's left?' I hear you say!

- Develop harmonic structure (fill out the chords) - mostly right hand stuff:
  Make good use of arpeggios and scales.
  Use more colourful chords than the basic triads - maybe learn some jazz chords. No one else will be playing in that space - it's all yours!

- Develop melodic structure, such as:

  Counter melody, Fills, Links, Introductions.

- Create smooth transitions using:

  Inversions of chords (look for shared notes between successive chords to minimise movement).

  Sustained chords, especially strings sounds.

- Create interesting textures using variety in voicings but beware of 'dense' sounds that come across as just mush when added to the other sounds through a PA.

- Learn to play from chord charts rather than written scores - it will give you a new-found freedom.

Bass

The bass guitar is in essence a rhythm instrument. It delivers rhythm spelt out with notes. Consequently, it should work very closely with the drummer or percussionist ('sitting' on the beats of the kick drum or snare).

- Aim for tight timing: Watch out for being late - anticipate the note to come. It is better to play the wrong note at the right time than the right note too late - better still to have the right note at the right time!

- Don't leave unintended gaps as they break up the rhythm.

- The bass line is often crucial to give the right shape and direction to a passage - a bass progression (e.g. D, A/C#, Bm, Bm/A, G).

- Bassists often have an obsession with not playing from music. This is fine if they know the song intimately. Start by encouraging them to actually learn the songs.

- Avoid musical cliches - simple underpinning of the chordal structure is very effective.

Drums

A drummer provides the rhythmic backbone of the band. Ideally, the whole band should follow the drums. In the case of developing a new drummer it might be prudent to have the band follow the leader - the guitarist or keyboard.

- A good back-beat is fine - there's no need for fancy stuff.

- Fancy stuff is only ok if it is absolutely in time (runs often tend to be late).

- Think about where you need to end up after a run, not exactly which beats you play.

- Make plenty of use of textural playing (e.g. gentle rolls with beaters on cymbals, subtle use of bigger toms etc).

- Suggest they practice with a metronome - to manage an even tempo throughout a song (since everyone else will probably speed up as things get louder).

Woodwind

A little here and there is definitely better than playing continuously - 'less is more'.

- Don't tootle away in the background.

- Consider scripting out some fills/links rather than 'improvise' (because it is difficult to do well).

- Use intervals other than 2nds (adjacent notes in the scale) to add interest, use bits of arpeggios.

Electric guitar

As with woodwind - 'less is more'.

- Watch the volume.

- Go easy on the distortion - it may sound great on stage but it will sound really muddy through a PA.

- Go for short, focused licks.

- When playing side guitar aim to develop and support the rhythm - don't cut across the lead instrument.

Vocals

A little effort here will pay huge dividends. This is the category where most people are likely to offer their services. Having a clear vision for how to develop vocalists improves skill levels very quickly.

Identify vocal roles:

- Lead - the tune, basically (some stylistic deviation can help add interest). This is what the congregation will follow, so make it clear and strong.

- Harmony - loose (go for interesting stuff)

- Melodic improvisation - ad lib singing around the tune, perhaps with suggested responses to the main lyrics.

- Core singing - reinforce the tune and close harmony.

General techniques:

- Aim for control - be precise in terms of pitch and timing.

- Think in terms of phrases (avoid breaking up sentences with breaths).

Make the sound as round and full as possible - avoid 'pure' choral tones - go for some character.

- Avoid cliches and over-stylised expressions (e.g. sliding into notes).
- Make use of dynamics (there are other volumes besides loud).
- 'Slenderise' the high notes (i.e. back off the volume and gracefully reach for the note).
- Be expressive - you're a story teller, not a news reader.

Positioning the Players

Aim for each 'category' to be represented - harmonic, rhythmic, melodic and vocals. This is easy if you have many instruments to work with. Often though, we have to build a band from a guitar, a violin, a flute and an oboe (or some such challenging combination). In this case it becomes very important to follow the above guidelines to focus the melodic instruments to avoid too much tootling. It would be worthwhile suggesting some people pick up new skills, say for the flautist to learn to play some percussion (tambourine, bongos, shaky eggs etc). This can often reveal much about people's hearts - whether they are there to serve or just to play things they enjoy. Setting aside personal preferences for the sake of the whole is something that gets regularly tested as a member of a worship band, whether it is not playing all the time or being asked to play a completely different instrument.

Learning a second or third instrument is generally much easier and quicker than the first. Once a reasonable level of musical experience has been gained in one instrument becoming proficient in another can happen in a few months and always benefits the person concerned. They see another view of the structure of music and are the richer for it.

10 Sound Reinforcement (PA)

Why Is It Needed?

Contemporary music and instruments (e.g. electric and bass guitars) need sound reinforcement. Volume (drums provide rhythm and uplift but easily overpower a voice and acoustic guitar 'unplugged'). The traditional choir achieves volume with numbers of voices; modern flexibility of worship leader and 2 vocalists needs amplification.

What system?

Music will not sound good through a set-up designed for speech reinforcement only. If a church is planning to grow, the future sound needs should be anticipated and a bigger system than presently necessary considered. It is a false economy to fit a system that will soon be 'out-grown'.

Sound systems and their installation are a costly process (but compare the installation of an organ and its upkeep). There will probably have to be a number of discussions at the right level (PCC, treasurer AGM etc) if a church is thinking of installing equipment for the first time. This takes time and the worship leader and band will have to be patient.

Too complex a system that cannot be run by present members of the congregation will be a white elephant. The prospective sound team need to be consulted. They may be willing to be trained, (this should be encouraged!) and they need to be willing and able to pass on their know-how and training to others in the congregation who have a technological bent and a musical ear.

Get professional advice, but don't be 'blinded by science'. Visit other churches in the area that have had sound systems fitted and take recommendations.

Some considerations

The worship band will probably be very keen to have a good system installed immediately! Some of them may already be playing in secular bands and be accustomed to the intricacies and the sight of the technology. The congregation may not be used to the sight of trailing leads, foldback speakers, microphones and amplifiers at the front of their church and may feel affronted by a sound system. The cost of an appropriate system may come as a surprise (shock!) to some.

This all calls for careful communication, explanation and consultation on the part of the church leader and patience on the part of the band.

Sound team - skills and qualifications

Technical know-how: Willingness and ability to learn from a more experienced team member, take instruction and correct mistakes.

Unflappability when things go wrong!

Musical ear: Know what the different instruments should sound like and what makes a good 'mix'. Probably listens to the style of music being played by the band and appreciates it.

A member of the worship team: Although positioned on their own at the sound desk, they need to be made to feel part of the team by praying together with the band, being at practices to experiment with sound, socialising with the band and being part of team training so that they are one with the vision for the worship.

Accountability: As part of the worship band they are accountable immediately to the worship leader, who in turn is accountable to the church leader. This means that requests from the congregation about volume should not be addressed to the sound desk but the leadership. (It is very disconcerting and confusing for the sound person to have various members of the congregation 'sneaking' back to them throughout a worship time to ask for the volume to be turned up or down. The person on sound needs to be able to say that they are under instructions from the worship leader and the church leader!)

The church leader takes responsibility for the church worship, so he can ask for the sound to be lowered 'front of house'. This may mean that the foldback speakers will also have to be turned down so that the sound at the front is not 'muddied'. This in turn may mean that the drummer will have to play 'down' so that the band is able to hear itself.

Reliability and punctuality: The sound person will need to arrive at church before the rest of the worship band in order to set up and check the system. If they are late the start of the whole service could be delayed!

Alertness: The sound person has to keep a constant eye on the proceedings at the front to make sure that the correct microphones are turned on for speech and music. When positioning a sound desk for the first time, ensure that the singers and leaders are visible to the person at the desk.

Both worship leader and church leader should thank and encourage the person on sound; they often go unnoticed at the back of the church - or they are only noticed when the system goes wrong!

Running a sound-check

Each instrument and voice needs to be checked for sound before the service begins. This will probably take half an hour or more. At the initial sound-check the band are under instructions from the sound desk and while the individual instruments are checked, the other players should pay attention and not 'twiddle' on their instruments. The worship leader shows his care for his sound person by keeping some order in the band!

Both foldback and then 'front of house' levels need to be set after this.

After the band has run through a verse or two of a song, the sound person checks with the band that the foldback level is satisfactory, making any necessary adjustments, before moving on to set the 'front of house' level (see appendix for more details).

If the church leader asks for the volume to be turned down and the sound check is still in progress, note that the band and sound person probably need to arrive earlier in future so that the preparation can be properly completed!

If there has been an unforeseen problem, explain this to the church leader. He may need to explain to the people beginning to gather for the service: e.g....'I'm sorry, we have had... the problem... with the sound this morning and we are trying to get the sound right as quickly as possible. We'd be grateful for your patience.'... There is no point in alienating the congregation at the outset; keep your perfectionist streak at bay on this occasion!

Remember that if a band is still doing a sound-check or loudly practising an unrehearsed song at full volume as the congregation is arriving for the service, it is unwelcoming and off-putting. A quieter level of worship will draw the worshippers in with greater expectation.

A more detailed description of running a sound system is included on page 57.

11 Criticism and how to deal with it.

Every leader (and worship band) gets criticism and no one enjoys it! However Paul encourages us to welcome it, as we can grow strong by handling it rightly. (2 Cor 12:10) The worship leader and their band are at the front of a spiritual battle (2 Chron 20:21) and receiving personal criticism is one of the ways they experience that.

Plan:

• Recognise the emotion of hurt and or anger. Talk to the Lord about it immediately.

• Know your own reactions. Withdrawal, defensiveness, aggression and depression can all be the result of receiving criticism.

• Guard against unholy responses. Bitter judgments, gossip, disloyalty, unkind or untrue words and hasty decisions ('I'm never playing again!'). We need to turn from these with the Lord's help.

• Seek help and counsel from a respected Christian, if the emotion and its effects do not subside.

• After the heat of the emotion has cooled, identify the source of the criticism. a) leader b) friend c) church member

• Decide whether it is constructive or destructive criticism. Constructive criticism helps you to improve in the long run, destructive criticism comes out of jealousy, resentment, pettiness and a bad relationship. Is there any reason for this breakdown that you could address?

Constructive criticism

• Invite it from those you respect, from your leader, from those you know love you.

• Pray about it.

• Talk it out with the giver and/or the church leader.

• Act on it where necessary.

You will need much encouragement as well!

Destructive criticism

- Beware of anonymous criticism ('a number of people think.....but I want to guard their confidentiality!').

- Beware of criticism said in your hearing but not to you.

- A worship leader is in a spiritual battle. Satan does not want the worship of God to flourish, so the worship leader is a prime target. Worship is a key weapon in this fight - God's presence is our fortress (Psalm 18:2).

- Repent quickly of any pride, blaming or hateful feelings.

- Live in your security as a child of God.

12 Singing in tongues

1Corinthians 14 is the only passage in the New Testament that throws much light on the subject of 'singing in tongues'. And even here Paul talks of 'speaking' in tongues as a way of praying (v.2,14,15) and singing 'with his spirit' as a way of praising God (v.15,16). There is obviously a way of singing and speaking with the mind and with the spirit (v.15). Praying and praising with the mind is using words understood by both user and hearer, whereas praying and praising with the spirit is not naturally understood by either.

Both ways of praying and praising were in evidence in the Corinthian church and we can assume that they were therefore heard elsewhere in the early church, because Paul seems to take the fact as a 'given'. It is the way that they are used that causes Paul concern, and so he has to address some issues that their use in the Corinthian church had thrown up. We can learn something from this.

First of all he clarifies the position:

• 'Tongues' edifies the individual believer as he worships God (v.2,4).

• 'Tongues' on their own do not edify the church (v.4,6).

• You can't hear and therefore understand the words, or follow a recognisable tune when believers are singing in tongues (v.6,7).

• Unbelievers, who may be present in public worship, will not understand singing in 'tongues' and may be quick to interpret it as 'crazy!' (v.23).

On the basis of this, Paul draws up the following suggestions:

• Do both in public worship - praying and praising with your spirit and your mind - but if you have sung in tongues makes sure you sing something intelligible too,(v.15) for the sake of other believers and unbelievers.

• In public worship the emphasis should be on using words understood by the people rather than using tongues (v.19) as that builds up the church. In other words spend more time singing with the mind than the spirit.

The fact that Paul has to 'ration' the use of tongues in the Corinthian church leads one to believe that it was being used too much there in his opinion. Possibly the balance of prayer and worship was more on 'tongues' than on plain language. He thought that the church would not thrive and would gain an unnecessarily bad reputation among unbelievers.

Nowadays the pendulum has swung so far the other way that it is possible to worship in church without ever being exposed to praying and praising 'with the spirit' - or even, in some cases, to know that such a thing exists and is desirable! For this reason, and because it is edifying to the believer, we need to teach about it.

What exactly is 'singing with the spirit'?

Singing with the spirit might be described as: singing to God using words or sounds which have not previously been written down as a song, or singing words in another language, unknown to the singer (tongues of angels or men). It includes singing these words in a tune which has also not been written up as a melody but which harmonises with all the other tunes that are being sung at the same time.

It may be very simple (one or two notes, one or two syllables). It may be complex, but the important thing is the singer's dedication to the Lord and availability to be inspired by God's Holy Spirit.

Is this something new?

There is good reason to believe that Christians have 'Sung in the Spirit' down through the last two millennium since the first outpouring of the Holy Spirit. Some think that the monks who sung what came to be known as Gregorian chants in the 9th Century modelled the sound of their singing on the pure and intoned sound of Christian groups singing in tongues. In 1567 Thomas Tallis wrote his now famous 40 part motet 'Spem in alium' (I Put My Trust In God) imitating the way many different voices blend to form one song of praise to God. Many who hear it are struck by the spiritual intensity of this work.

When should we sing in the Spirit?

The best time to sing in the spirit is when a group is focused on the truth of who God is, and His love for the believer. For this reason it is usually good to lead a time of worship by declaring the truth about God first, using songs that most people are familiar with.

A good worship leader looks and listens, to see how tired or harassed, or alternatively expectant and full of faith the worshipping group is at the beginning. Choose songs accordingly. Tired people don't necessarily want to learn the latest 'hot' song, but songs that they know and like will remind them of God's goodness and draw them into praise and worship.

Learning a new song focuses the attention on the song and, because they do not know it, people tend to sing tentatively. Neither of these things is a good preparation for singing in the Spirit, - unless people are very quick to pick up the song and are very used to singing in tongues!

You will probably need to lead 3 or 4 songs before people are ready to sing in tongues or in the spirit.

There are 2 classic ways to start singing in the spirit:

1.When people are caught up in the presence of the Lord, singing their hearts out, keep the momentum up at the end of the song (ie don't slow down and sing more quietly) and then continue it by singing in tongues. Keep your instruments playing in the same one chord at the end of the song (beforehand, encourage other band members to stick to the same chord range). As the people join in, and the song swells, encourage the group to sing whatever is on their hearts to the Lord. 'You may want to sing in English or in a tongue that the Holy Spirit gives you' (This gives any outsider in the group some reassurance that their neighbour singing loudly in tongues is doing something you expect...!) When you judge it appropriate, you could return to the chorus of the song you have previously sung (it should all still be in the right key!).

2. When there is a real sense of the Lord's nearness, the singing often dies away as worshippers experience the holiness and intimacy of the Lord's presence. At the end of such a song you may need some moments of silence out of which you can lead singing in the spirit. As the one voice starts to sing, others may join in singing to the Lord. Allow people to sing unaccompanied at this point so that you can hear the harmony of voices. It may continue as a 'murmur'. The instruments may want to join in after a while but should be careful not to overpower the voices. Don't be afraid of leaving people in silence at the end. You can put them at ease by saying something simple like, 'lets spend a few moments in silence before the Lord.'

At the end of a worship time when you have sung in tongues, it can be helpful to give a brief explanation of what was happening for the benefit of newcomers. Encourage any (puzzled) believers that this is for them and they can join in next time! You may want to reassure them that it is not necessary for everyone to be involved in it, but anyone can ask for this gift! It may be appropriate to find out if people want to testify afterwards to what the Lord has done during the worship time. It is encouraging for the whole group to know if the Lord has spoken to someone, healed or restored etc.

Remember Paul's admonition to the Corinthians not to get so excited and 'carried away' that they *only* worship by singing 'with the spirit'!

13 Songwriting

Matt Redman

Matt Redman is one of the most prolific songwriters of this generation. His songs of worship are sung around the world, finding echoes in the hearts of worshippers of all ages and cultures. He started to write his own songs for use in his church, because they expressed what God was doing in their hearts and lives. This can really add something to the worship of a local church. Here he shares some of his thoughts and inspiration:

The starting point

Jesus told us that 'out of the overflow of the heart the mouth speaks.' And it's the same with writing, singing and making music to the Lord - all the best stuff happens when it's truly the overflow of our hearts. The King James translation actually says 'Out of the abundance of the heart' - again it conjures up a great picture of having so much love in our hearts for God that we can hardly keep it in. That's the starting point with songwriting.

Finding inspiration

Make sure it's not just some clever words put together with a nice tune. A meaningful song will always be the passionate expression of your heart towards God. For that reason I personally don't find it very easy to say, 'OK, I'm going to write a song on holiness today' for example. It needs to be something burning in me - something that God's doing in my life or the life of our church that I want to respond to Him on. In a sense this is the initial inspiration side - a little seed that God has planted in your heart that will grow into a song. But it may need nurturing.

The hard work factor

This is the 'perspiration' side. Sometimes you hear a song and it's got a lot of heart, but it doesn't sound like it's been worked on at all. It is meaningful, but doesn't feel like it's been finished and made ready for congregational use. All inspiration and not much perspiration.

Other times you'll hear a song and it has lots of words, perfect rhymes and a singable tune, yet not much heart. It feels like there's been a lot of perspiration, but it's missing that vital inspiration factor.

The best songs have both - a mixture of heartfelt inspiration that has been carefully crafted for congregational use.

Finding a subject

The most helpful thing I ever heard about songwriting was from Brian Doerkson of the Vineyard. He said that a good song expresses a 'universal theme in a unique way'. I always try to remember that. We're trying to write a song around a theme that people can relate to and will want to sing about. But we're trying to express it in a fresh new way, musically and lyrically, so it comes alive in our hearts.

i. The Bible

The best starting place is obviously the Bible. There can be a temptation to just look in the Psalms for inspiration - that's an obvious place, but actually there's a wealth of ideas waiting for you all over the Bible. I often find a certain verse somewhere will stand out to me. It feels like revelation - perhaps a great poetic line of love for God, or perhaps a fresh way of describing who He is.

For example, recently I was trying to write a little love song to God, but couldn't find that 'unique' way. Then I stumbled across a verse in Ecclesiastes 5 which said 'God is in heaven, and you are on earth, so let your words be few'. For me that was the seed of the song..... 'Let my words be few'. There's a time to love God with many words, but there's also a time to come before Him with the fewest of words and the simplest of songs. The passage goes on to say, 'Therefore stand in awe of God', and that became the chorus of the song. A few verses from the Bible, which I'd probably read through before, helped me in that moment give fresh expression to the worship that was stirring in my heart for God.

ii. Old hymn books

As lyric writers we need to keep our antennae up - being aware wherever we are or whatever we're doing for little lines or ideas that may be the seed of song. As I said the Bible is by far the most obvious, but it doesn't stop there. I've found inspiration by reading through old hymn books, for example. A fresh theme or lyric from a hymn often helps me glimpse a new angle on God or the way we worship Him.

iii. Talks and seminars

Sometimes in a talk the speaker will say a phrase that strikes you as fresh and inspires you. Note it down and turn it over in your mind in the following days.

iv. Life events

Perhaps God is doing something in your life, or the life of your church. A few years back I had a phone call to say that my Grandfather was in hospital and was going to die the next day. As far as I'm aware, he didn't know the Lord, and was the first person close to me to die who didn't. I started to sing out to God on my guitar, thinking about whether it was too late for my Grandfather. Then my thoughts went wider: Is it too late for a nation? Can a nation be saved? It turned into a little song which helped me grieve my Grandfather, but also intercede for a nation who didn't know God. It was the overflow of my heart at that particular moment.

v. Church life

As songwriters it can be great when we reflect on what God is doing in the lives of our churches in any particular season. It's good to keep open to and aware of any themes that arise from a sermon, or even from a prophetic word during the service, and then capture the essence of that theme in a song responding to the Lord.

Making the most of the moment

We need to be ready to give expression to these things. Often I might be out or in the car and I'll have a little tune/lyric idea I don't want to forget, so as soon as I can I'll write it down, or sing it down a phone onto my answer machine at home. I've got a folder full of scraps of paper with little lyric ideas on. It's amazing how often they'll come in handy when you're finding it hard to finish another song!

The craft

Take time. Sometimes ideas will stir in our hearts for a while before we manage to express them in the way we want to. Once the inspiration is there, it's important to find time and space for the perspiration side of things. Sometimes I've rewritten a chorus ten times because I know it's still not expressing exactly what God is stirring in my heart.

Be ruthless. It's important to be ruthless. Maybe there's a lyric that was only put in because it rhymes, or maybe you've got a melody note that, realistically, is too high for people to sing. At that point it's important to not just think, 'O, that will do...', but to be ruthless. There's usually a way round all these little obstacles that come our way, as we learn the craft of writing congregational songs.

Constructive criticism. Surround your self with some support. We're often not the best judges of our own songs, and it's good to find one or two people who can help you critique it constructively. They don't have to be musicians necessarily, but it is important they understand about worship. Ask them if the words make sense, and if it's singable. Ask them what the weakest point is (often they'll confirm your worst suspicions on a part of the song you knew wasn't finished properly!). Hopefully they'll encourage you too!

Let's write!

As someone who leads worship regularly at my church, I know what a difference a new song can make to the worship times, Often fresh songs unlock freshness in our worship times together. Of course bring in songs from the outside, but be encouraged to write songs that spring up from within the heart of a congregation. That can be a really precious thing - a home-grown song that reflects your congregation's journey with God.

Let's get serious about writing our love songs for God - songs that will touch His heart, glorify His name, and be a resource for our churches as they seek to do the same.

Conclusion

'Its all about Jesus' is the refrain of a popular worship song and we would do well to remember that in all the organisation, preparation, conflict-resolution, arranging, composing, paying for and playing of our worship, the Lord Jesus Christ is the one and only focus, end and meaning to it all.

If He receives the worship of *my heart* there is nothing and no-one outside of me that can stop me worshipping Him. I can worship Him wherever I am - with the great congregation in church, or alone in my room; in freedom, or in prison ; in the worship band, or in the congregation; with my family, or in my broken marriage; single or married; musical or tone-deaf.

I need not wait until my circumstances change before I express the love in my heart for Him.

I need not wait until my musical gifting is more refined or better acknowledged before I let Him know that I adore Him.

I need not wait until my church is expressing its worship in a more up-to-date and lively way before I bring Him my worship.

The only thing that will stop me worshipping Jesus is filling my heart with something or someone else above Him. Even the mechanics of our worship can become a hindrance to a relationship of love and obedience to Jesus. Many think that Satan was originally a worship leader in heaven, highly gifted in creative arts and 'full of wisdom and perfect in beauty' (Ezekiel 28:12) He was blameless till 'wickedness was found in you' (v.15) The underlying cause of this wickedness is seen in verse 17: 'Your heart became proud on account of your beauty, and you corrupted your wisdom because of your splendour.'

The worship of God is such a central and sacred task that it has been a prime focus of Satan's attack ever since. If he can get us to follow him on the road to pride, he has won a great victory. We need to be constantly alert to the dangers of pride in our worship;-

our band is better than the other;

I'm a better worship leader and should be playing for the 'big' service;

the song I wrote is the one that should be sung;

no-one tells me how to play/lead/sing;

the way that church does worship is laughable;

I should be playing this big instrumental solo;

I'm too important/busy a worship leader now to lead worship for that little group;

All these sentiments, and others like them, can creep in unawares if we allow them and they will ruin us and our worship. I often pray a prayer that runs like this 'Use me or lay me aside but glorify your name Lord Jesus'.

One day we will all gather around the throne of heaven and join in the eternal voice of praise and worship - it will be gloriously spectacular! Until then we are just practising for eternity - let's give the Lord Jesus the best we can!

Appendix
Operating a Sound System

The following extracts are taken from the PA operator's handbook compiled by Andy Rushton for use at St Barnabas, Woodside Park, London. While some of this therefore may be specific, we hope that these passages are of sufficiently general interest to be included:

St Barnabas' P.A. Mission Statement

The P.A. system exists to serve three groups of people:

The Congregation:

     a) To make audible everything that happens on-stage,

     b) To help create a comfortable worship environment.

The Service Leader and Speaker:

     a) To enable the service to be clearly directed,

     b) To allow the message to be communicated effectively.

The Worship Band:

     a) To amplify instruments and voices as necessary to meet the needs of the congregation,

     b) To ensure that the worship leader can be heard clearly on-stage,

     c) To enable the musicians to hear their own and others' instruments.

Section-by-Section on the Mixing Desk

The mixing desk is the heart of the P.A. system. It controls the volume of each microphone and instrument and allows us to adjust the sound quality. Through it we can also play music and video, as well as control the overall sound levels in the church. The mixing desk is probably the most intimidating part of the system.

a) Gain Controls

The most important controls on the desk are the gain controls. These control the volume (gain) of the signal from each microphone and instrument as it comes into the mixing desk. If this control is set too low, it will be difficult to hear that particular channel in the overall mix, no matter how high the fader is pushed. If it is set too high, the channel will overload and distort (the 'peak' light flashes to indicate this is happening).

b) E.Q. Controls

The four E.Q. (equalisation) controls shape the quality of the sound as it passes through the desk. Each control affects a particular frequency, and can make that frequency louder or quieter. The frequencies that we have control over are Bass, Low mid, High mid, and High.

c) Foldback

The foldback system is like a second P.A., for the benefit of the musicians. Without it, the singers would find it difficult to hear themselves over the drums, and the worship leader would have a hard time directing the band. The foldback mix is of vital importance to the musicians - they play much better if they can hear themselves and each other.

To improve the foldback mix, the P.A. operator must listen to it - on stage! This is the only way to get an accurate picture of the volume of the foldback compared to that of the unamplified instruments. The mix should be just loud enough for the musicians to be able to hear their own instrument or voice. The worship leader (and his/her instrument) should be clearly audible all over the stage.

Instruments not requiring foldback:

> Drums (!)
>
> Bass Guitar
>
> Any guitar with its own on-stage amplifier/speaker

d) Monitoring

Monitoring means checking the levels of the signal, using the meters, and listening to the sound as it passes through the desk, using the headphones provided. It is important to stress that listening to the sound from the speakers results in the best mix, and the operator should minimise the time spent using the headphones.

We can monitor the sound at several points as it travels through the mixing desk:

1) PFL (pre-fade listen)

Select 'PFL' from the monitor controls, then select one channel's 'PFL' button. The sound from that channel (before it passes through the fader) will be audible in the headphones. Adjust the 'monitor' volume control if necessary.

2) Foldback

We can listen to the signal being sent to the singers and/or the musicians' foldback, although it is far more useful to listen to the sound of these foldback mixes on-stage.

3) Mono

This is the signal that is sent to the amplifiers - it can occasionally be useful to hear the whole mix in this way. Monitoring individual instruments or voices using 'PFL' is important for setting gain levels, as already described. It is also useful for setting up the E.Q., as we can compare the sound of the instrument or voice unamplified with the sound that the P.A. is picking up and adjust the E.Q. accordingly.

Remember that most people will hear a combination of the original, unamplified sound of the music as well as the sound coming from the speakers. This is why it is impossible to create a really good mix with headphones on - we become unaware of the sound that people are really hearing!

Ancillary Equipment

(This section describes the pieces of equipment that may be attached to the P.A. desk).

a) Playback. To play cassette tapes, CDs and videos through the P.A. system

b) Recording. To record services, sermons, prayers etc.

c) Talkback. The talkback facility enbles the P.A.operator to communicate with the musicians on-stage without having to shout or leave the P.A. desk.

d) Reverb. Reverb can be added to the sound arriving at any channel. For the uninitiated, a touch of reverb will add a 'professional' sound to any singer, will cause thin-sounding instruments to fatten up, and can make a snare drum sound huge. Only certain instruments will benefit from having reverb added to the sound.

Use reverb with: Vocals. Flute/Strings. Acoustic guitars - use with care, as you can 'muddy' the rhythms of the guitarist. Piano - only if the pianist has no reverb added to their sound. Drums - snare drum only.

Do not use reverb with: Any microphone used for speech. Any bass instrument (kick drum, bass guitar). Any instrument that already has its own reverb (elec. guitar, synth).

Microphones

We use several types of microphone for different applications. These are the main types:

1.Radio Tieclip

Used sometimes by the service leader and always by the main speaker, the radio tieclip is a small, condenser-type microphone, which is connected to a radio transmitter

2.Lectern Microphone

Another condenser-type mic. Condensers are more fragile than dynamic microphones (so try to discourage people from getting too close when speaking into it) but are more sensitive, and will pick up a great deal of sound around them.

3. Dynamic Microphones

We have a range of dynamic microphones available,including Shure SM58, SM57 etc. We try to give the best quality mic to the worship leader - usually an SM58. Which is the best depends on, amongst other things, how often a particular mic has been dropped recently...

4. Radio Handheld Microphone

This mic uses a radio transmitter, in a similar way to the tieclip, but is a dynamic, rather than a condenser, mic. We use rechargeable 9-volt batteries to power the transmitter, a fresh one of which needs to be installed in the handheld mic before the start of each service.

D.I. Boxes

A D.I. (Direct-inject) box is a device to convert a signal directly from a guitar or electric piano into the right sort of signal for a P.A. system. Any instrument that has a 'jack' plug (1/4 inch) output needs to be plugged into a D.I. box, and the box is then itself plugged into one of the inputs on the stage boxes.

Step-by-Step on a typical Sunday

1. Stage Setup

The P.A. operator needs to be at the Church about an hour before the start of the service, in order to have enough time to set up and sound check. The first job is to prepare the stage for the band. Often, an operator will work consistently with the same group of musicians, and will know their needs from previous experience. However occasionally, we will be mixing a group for the first time, so it's sometimes worth contacting the worship leader beforehand to discuss the band's requirements.

a) Drums

The drum kit should be set up towards the back of the stage, and slightly to one side. The bass (kick) drum should be angled off-centre; this reduces the effect of 'standing waves' or echoes when the drum is played loudly.

b) Bass Guitar

The bass has its own amplifier on-stage. The bass player will plug into the amp, and set a sound that he or she is happy with. However, the bass player cannot sit in the body of the church to hear what the bass sounds like out there, and it is up to the P.A. operator to point out if, from this position, the bass is either too loud, or the wrong frequencies are boosted on the amp's graphic E.Q. Both these situations occur frequently, so be tactful!

c) Keyboard

d) Lead Guitar

The lead, or electric, guitarists invariably bring their own on-stage amplifier to the service, and will set it up themselves

e) Vocal Microphones

f) Other Microphones

2. Initial Sound check

The purpose for the initial sound check:

a) To get all the microphones and instruments

     1. working

     2. giving their optimum performance

     In order to test whether this is the case, it is necessary to have a signal coming through each channel. Ideally, we would have each instrument play on its own, at maximum volume. It is then easy to check if it is working, and to set the gain control to the optimum position.

Do not be distracted during this part of the sound check by requests from others. You must get this part of the job right in order to get a good sound, and it is necessary to do it first. If the band start asking for fine adjustments to the foldback mix, explain that you will see to it in a moment. (Although they will need to be able to hear the worship leader in the foldback throughout the rehearsal).

3. Foldback Sound check

Once again, it must be stressed that only by walking to the platform and listening to the sound on-stage as the band are playing can you properly assess the foldback mixes, and the exercise is good for you!

The band must be consulted individually.

a) The most common complaint is 'I can't hear the worship leader!', and this could mean either the leader's vocal mica, or the leader's instrument. Find out which, and turn it up on the appropriate foldback mix .

b) The next most common cry - 'I can't hear myself !' It's important to remember that individual instruments and voices should not be turned up louder than the worship leader (otherwise they will become the worship leader!).

NB However loud you turn up the mix on-stage, a musician will have problems hearing it if they are nowhere near a monitor speaker. Make sure that each musician is as close as practicable to a monitor (it's easier to move the monitors rather than the musicians).

And finally, two important points:

a) The foldback mix is for the musicians only and, ideally, should not be heard at all by the congregation. The louder this mix is, the less control you will have over the resulting sound in the main building. Once the mix is to everyone's satisfaction, try to reduce the volume levels on-stage. The drummer may have to play a little more quietly as a result, but there will be a big increase in sound quality out front.

b) The foldback level is affected by the gain controls - if you carefully set the foldback mix then readjust the gains, your foldback mix will change as well, and you'll have to start from the beginning. This is why you must set the gain controls first, before dealing with the musicians' on-stage needs.

4. E.Q. Fine-tuning

General Hints for using E.Q. controls:

Cut rather than boost frequencies, if possible. Adding high frequencies in particular can mean increased hiss.

Don't cut or boost all the frequencies at once - it's unlikely to improve the sound.

Start with the controls at the centre (no boost/cut) position, then gently sweep to either side until you hear the result you desire.

5. Speech Mic Sound check

The last thing to do before the service, after the band has finished the sound check, is to check that all the speech mikes are in working order

6. Working the Mix

Be ready.

The service is about to begin. At this point you need to be particularly aware of what is happening at the front of the church - be ready! The service leader will want to welcome the congregation. The service leader will not want to stand there like a lemon while you finish your conversation, put down your cup of tea, find the correct fader and fade it up!

The first song.

Try to allow the words to come over strongly, if you can. Remember that the worship leader needs to be heard by the congregation.

As you begin to mix the music, you will notice something strange. Your carefully set balance has changed since the sound check. Instruments that were clearly audible can no longer be heard, voices sound muffled and distant, even through the P.A. This is because of the MABs, or Mobile Acoustic Baffles. Otherwise known as people, each MAB will absorb some of the sound that the P.A. puts out (around 2-4Watts' worth), but they won't soak up all the frequencies evenly, so the mix doesn't just sound quieter, it sounds different.

1. Turn up the music to compensate for the sound being absorbed.

2. Review all of your E.Q. settings in the light of this new sound environment.

Vocals audible? - Try turning up the hi-mid for a brighter sound.

Instruments clear? - Use the E.Q. to separate out instruments further if necessary.

Volume.

Use common sense when setting volume levels, but there are two things to bear in mind that should help you to achieve a good level:

a) Try to mix the sound according to the direction the worship leader is taking. If the song is an upbeat, clappy one, turn it up. If it's a reflective song, keep it down. It's unlikely that one volume level will be suitable throughout the worship time, so you must keep reviewing how loud the music actually is.

Which brings us on to the second point;

b) You do not hear what everyone else hears. Most of the congregation are closer to a speaker than you are, most of them will be experiencing higher SPLs (sound pressure levels) than you. Especially those right next to any bass bins. It is vital that you are aware of how your adjustments on the desk affect everyone in the building, and here the advice is the same as it was for the foldback mix: go listen to it!

7. Winding Up

Towards the end of the service we often have a ministry time, led by the service leader and accompanied by the band. There are two adjustments that we can make to the settings on the desk that will facilitate this period of the service.

1. Turn down the level of the foldback

2. Add the speech mikes into the foldback mix, enabling the band and, particularly, the worship leader to hear spoken instructions from whoever is leading the service at that point.

New Wine Vision

We want to see as many Christians and Churches as possible alive with the joy of knowing and worshipping Jesus Christ, and equipped to live out and proclaim his Kingdom in the love of God the Father, and the power and gifts of the Holy Spirit.

New Wine Mission

Through the Holy Spirit, we seek fulfilment of this vision through:

• Summer Family Conferences. These events aim to envision and empower Christians and Churches for worship which is passionate, intimate, reverent and biblical; for ministry in the power and gifts of the Spirit, modelled in a mature, responsible way; and through Bible expositions and a breadth of seminar options, to equip them for Spirit-filled Christian life and ministry.

• The work of the New Wine Networks. Providing relational support and encouragement for like-minded leaders across the UK and other nations. Regional training conferences (1-3 days in length) are held all around the networks. We also place strategic emphasis on training church leaders through a programme of leadership training conferences, and the New Wine Leaders' Retreats.

• Encouraging faith-sharing visits to churches that are seeking to grow in renewal by leaders and other teachers taking out teams of people from their churches.

• Discerning where the Spirit is leading in issues of social responsibility, justice, community and the environment.

• Encouraging Church Planting.

• Publishing: New Wine Magazine, books and other teaching materials (eg video and audio cassette material) as a further means of propagating teaching which adheres to New Wine values.

In this work we have an especial, though not exclusive, concern for the Church of England, from which New Wine emerged, and other traditional Churches.

New Wine – equipping churches to extend Jesus' Kingdom.

New Wine, 4a Ridley Avenue, Ealing, London W13 9XW
Tel: 020 8567 6717 Fax: 020 8840 4735
Email: info@new-wine.org Web Site: www.new-wine.org